MARGARET CLARK
Illustrated by David Pearson

To Nick, Selina, Elliot, and Thomas

Written by Margaret Clark
Illustrated by David Pearson
Designed by Peter Shaw

Published by Mimosa Publications Pty Ltd
PO Box 779, Hawthorn 3122, Australia
© 1995 Mimosa Publications Pty Ltd
All rights reserved

Literacy 2000 is a Trademark registered in the United States Patent and Trademark Office.

Distributed in the United States of America by
RIGBY
A Division of Reed Elsevier Inc.
PO Box 797
Crystal Lake, IL 60039-0797
800-822-8661

Distributed in Canada by
GINN PUBLISHING CANADA INC.
3771 Victoria Park Avenue
Scarborough
Ontario M1W 2P9

99 98 97 96 95
10 9 8 7 6 5 4 3 2 1
Printed in Hong Kong through Bookbuilders Ltd

ISBN 0 7327 1569 5

CONTENTS

1. Me and My Big Mouth 5
2. Making Money 11
3. Accidental Emergency 27
4. Flower Power 35
5. Out of Luck 41
6. Hairy's Friend 53

CHAPTER 1

Getting a grip on life is not easy. Having a name like Pip doesn't help. (It's short for Philippa, and that's even worse!) Having Peppercorn as a last name doesn't help. Being eleven years, five months, and eleven days old doesn't help. Being the only girl in my family doesn't help, and nor does having zillions of freckles. And having a fiery temper helps even less.

"Who left all these soggy cotton balls in the bathroom?" says Dad, walking into the kitchen while I'm setting the table.

"Pip's been putting lemon juice on her freckles again," says Chris, my motormouth brother, who sometimes just can't mind his own business, "but I don't know why she bothers. If you're as freckly as she is, you need a new face."

"That's enough," says Dad, but it's too late. I've already picked up a big lemon from the fruit bowl and yelled, "This is for you, Chris! A lemon for a lemon head!"

What I want to know is why he didn't try to catch it! That's what he was supposed to do. But instead he just ducks! The next second there's an ear-splitting crash as the lemon smashes through the kitchen window and lands, splat, all over Dad's car parked in the driveway.

I can't believe it. My fourth window in two months: one from a baseball, one from my frisbee, one from a soccer ball – and now a lemon. It's not funny, but I start to giggle. I often do that when I'm upset, and it usually gets me into more trouble.

"Now you've done it, freckle brain," says Chris, grinning.

Dad's angrier than a wasp in a bottle.

"That's it," he says. "You can pay for this window yourself."

ME AND MY BIG MOUTH

GET A GRIP, PIP!

"But the last three times the insurance paid," says Chris.

Thanks a lot, budget brain, I think. Did you have to remind Dad that this is the fourth time?

"This is the fourth time, Pip," says Dad. "This was willful damage. The other three were accidents. Therefore, you will be doing whatever jobs need to be done around here every afternoon and all weekend for the next two weeks to earn enough money to pay for the damage. And you can clean up that mess on my car before dinner."

"That's not fair," I say. "I didn't mean to break the window. It wasn't willful damage at all. Chris was supposed to catch it."

Dad is unmoved.

"How can I pay for the window? I'm still paying off the quilt," I say desperately. The quilt wasn't my fault, either. My friend Becky spilled "Scarlet Dreamtime" all over it when we were experimenting with her sister's nail polish.

"Add it on to the national Pip Peppercorn debt," says Chris.

He can talk! If he had caught the lemon like he was supposed to, I wouldn't be in this trouble. "It's not fair," I shout, stomping my

8

foot in frustration. "You're being too hard on me. I'm only a kid."

"Get a grip on yourself, Pip," answers Dad. "You threw the lemon. You have to take the consequences. Now go and wash that mess off my car."

I go out with a bucket and sponge and start washing. It's impossible. I'll never be able to earn enough in two weeks to pay all these debts. At this rate, I'll be paying stuff off until I'm a hundred. They'll be taking it out of my social security.

But the money is only one part of what's worrying me. The worst thing is, this has happened on the worst possible day. I can see it all so clearly: the school principal, Mr. Blitheroe, announcing at assembly that for the next two weeks our school is taking part in a charity drive to raise money for needy kids. There are prizes, too – a new computer for the school that raises the most money and, even better than that, a special plaque for the most successful individual.

It really fired my imagination. I wanted to help those kids, and winning that plaque would show Dad that I could do more than just get into trouble. So, of course, I let it slip out that I was going to raise the most money, and I said it loud enough for the whole school to hear.

But I'll be lucky to pay off my debt in two weeks, let alone raise any money for charity. Me and my big mouth! What am I going to do?

CHAPTER 2

MAKING MONEY

I've slept on my problem, but things don't look a whole lot better when I wake up in the morning. The only good news is that it's Saturday, I don't have to go to school, and I'm one day closer to being twelve.

One big problem about being eleven years, five months, and twelve days old is that there isn't a lot of scope for making money, even when it's Saturday and I've got all day. If I wash Dad's car, he'll probably knock a few dollars off my hundred-and-fifty-dollar debt. Big deal. But it's better than nothing, so I start.

"Hi, Pip."

It's Corey, the kid from next door. He's only five and he's kind of cute; it's just that he likes to follow me everywhere, which can be a real pain. But his mother's really nice. She waves from their yard and I wave and smile back so that she knows I don't mind Corey coming over.

"What're you doing, Pip?"

"I'm taking helicopter lessons," I say, as I slosh more sudsy water over the car.

"Where's the helicopter? I don't see any helicopter. Why are...?"

It's too hard. Why did I ever try to crack a joke with a five-year-old brain? Then I get inspiration. "Here, Corey," I say. "You can be my Hubcap-Washing Robot."

"Oh, wow!" Corey grabs a cloth and starts washing wheels. Black gunk splatters all over him but he's actually having fun – plus I won't have to do the wheels myself. Maybe he'll do a few more of the dirtier jobs if I make them sound important.

"Control to Robot," I say, "here's a nice, soft rag to polish up the chrome."

"Shame on you," says Dad, who's on his way to the garage. "Now you can pay Corey for helping you, Pip, seeing as how you're subcontracting him."

MAKING MONEY

Isn't anything ever going to start going right? How on earth can I pay Corey when I don't have any money? Is this Let's-All-Hate-Pip week? And paying a five-year-old to slosh around in a bucket and get filthy dirty when he's left the hubcaps streaky isn't my idea of social justice, either.

"Help, Pip! Help!"

Now what? I turn around from washing the windshield and there's a big, brown dog with a gigantic pink tongue, and it's licking Corey's face.

"It's okay, Corey." I point to the dog's tail, which is wagging like a helicopter's rotor. "He wants to be friends." I put down my rag and bend down next to Corey. The dog tries to lick my face, and I notice a round tag on his collar.

"Howard," I read aloud. "32 Finch Street. Phone 555-4811. Well, Howard," I say to the dog, "this isn't 32 Finch Street. That's five blocks away. I think you're lost." Howard puts a dopey look on his face and wags his tail even harder.

"Tell you what," I say to him, "you stay here and mind Corey and I'll call your owner."

I go inside and try, but the phone is busy so I go back outside to check that I've got the right number. Howard's lying on his back with his legs in the air while Corey tickles his tummy, and I can't get anywhere near his collar to look. It will be quicker to walk him home at this rate.

"Dad, I'm walking a dog home. I'll only be half an hour," I call, as I find some rope.

"Have you finished the car?"

"Yeah."

"And put everything away?"

MAKING MONEY

I tie Howard up to the drainpipe while I put away the hose and the buckets. Corey wanders inside. Just when I'm ready to go, our cat, Meatball, appears around the corner, sees Howard, and starts arching her back and spitting. Howard immediately goes into I-Hate-Cats mode, tries to get at Meatball, and strains wildly against the rope as Meatball dashes up the apple tree. The drainpipe gives a creak and starts to part company from the wall.

"Oh, no!" I quickly untie Howard, who's suddenly got the strength of a bull elephant, tie him around the base of the apple tree, and shove the drainpipe back against the wall. Unless you look closely you can't see that it's just sort of leaning there. Now I'm hoping that it doesn't rain for about five years – at least until I've made enough money to pay off all my other debts.

GET A GRIP, PIP!

"Come on, you big slob," I say to Howard as I untie him, "let's get you back home." He pulls like mad against the rope. I can read his mind. It says: "CAT." Then Corey comes trotting out with a handful of cookies.

"There's no dog food," he says, giving them to Howard, who wags his tail in ecstasy.

"He'll get sick," I say, horrified. I don't know a lot about dogs, but I'm sure they're not supposed to guzzle five cookies in one big gulp.

"Come on, Howard. Home."

"I want to come, too," says Corey. He's got that look on his face that means he's going to scream if I don't let him tag along.

So we go and ask his Mom. She says that it's okay, and she tells Corey to be good. So do I.

"Okay. I'll be good. Can I hold the rope?"

We take off out the gate with Howard dragging Corey at top speed down the street. I'm praying that we get Howard safely home and that he doesn't suddenly collapse with some kind of cookie-induced illness. But Howard seems perfectly fine – he's on the homeward trail and picking up speed. Then suddenly he stops dead, throwing Corey off balance, and we're outside 32 Finch Street.

GET A GRIP, PIP!

I open the wooden latticed gate and we walk up the path. Corey holds Howard while I ring the bell. A lady opens the door and Howard launches himself at her. "Where was he?" she asks, so I explain what happened.

"He's been missing for two days," she says. "He must be starving."

I'm not so sure about that. I think he's had a few free meals along the way.

MAKING MONEY

"Here's your reward," she says, and gives me ten dollars.

"That's okay. We didn't want a reward. We're happy he's home safe and well, aren't we, Corey?"

"Take the money," she insists. "Buy yourselves a treat or go to the movies."

Next thing we know, we're out in the street clutching the ten dollars.

"Great," says Corey. "Can we see *Ol' Bug Eyes*? I've heard it's cool."

How does a five-year-old kid know about "cool" movies? I look at the ten dollars. What if I returned ten lost dogs – I'd have a hundred dollars! It's easier and more fun than washing cars. My brain starts ticking with ideas.

"Are we going to see the movie now?" asks Corey.

"Not now," I say.

"Why not?"

"Because we're going to be much too busy returning lost dogs. We'll be partners and make lots of money. You've heard about Neighborhood Watch. Well, we'll be Dog Watch."

"Okay. Where are the lost dogs?"

Corey has a point there. We go to the park, but all the dogs there are attached to owners. We walk along some streets, quietly calling, "Here, dog" and "Come on, pooch" – just in case there are any dogs loose that might like to let us find them.

MAKING MONEY

But the only dogs we see are definitely *un*-lost, and safe behind fences. Except (and this is when I get an idea) there's a cute, little, shaggy brown dog trying to squash itself to the size of a pancake to squeeze its way to freedom. I call, "Here, pooch." Maybe if this dog "escapes" I can return it to its owners when they get home.

"He's not lost," says Corey.

"He might be," I say, even though my heart is beating so hard that I know I don't really believe it. I'm starting to think this wasn't such a good idea after all.

GET A GRIP, PIP!

Then a lady appears and calls, "Tootsie! Who's that upsetting you?"

Now I'm convinced this was a bad idea. Time to bail out!

It's almost lunchtime and all we have is ten dollars for finding Howard. We stop at the store on the way home and buy drinks and a large bag of jelly beans. I wrap the change safely in the handkerchief I have in my pocket, and tuck the jelly beans into Corey's pocket for later.

"Remember, Dog Watch is a big secret, Corey," I remind him as we arrive back home. "If you tell, no jelly beans. It's up to you."

And there's Dad, just getting out of his car. "Where have you two been?" he snaps, looking grim.

"I told you I was taking Corey with me," I say, stalling for time.

"What have you been up to? You have a very suspicious look on your face, young lady. And what happened to that half hour you mentioned?"

I can never understand how Dad knows when I've been doing something I shouldn't, or even *thinking* about doing something I shouldn't. It's like he's got some sort of built-in radar in his brain. He's warming up to total aggravation. His nostrils are sort of wiggling and his hazel eyes are narrowing into slits.

"We went for a walk," I say. Well, we *did* go for a walk. It's true.

GET A GRIP, PIP!

"Chris has had an accident," says Dad. "I had to take him to hospital and leave him there waiting for the results of his X-rays while I came back to the house..." he pauses to let guilt seep in to my brain, "to find out if you and Corey had come back."

Corey just looks at his shoes. But I want to know what's happened to Chris. Has he fallen off his skateboard again? Has he electrocuted himself playing around on his computer? "What's happened to Chris?" I ask.

"Something upset poor Meatball. She was right at the top of the apple tree, meowing and wailing, and she wouldn't come down."

Oops! I'd forgotten all about Meatball.

MAKING MONEY

"So," Dad continues explaining, "Chris got a ladder and climbed up the tree. Meatball leaped onto the roof, and just as he went to grab her, the drainpipe gave way. He's got a possible broken wrist, and also possible concussion. Get in the car, Pip. And Corey, you'll have to come with us. Your mom's gone out, so we're watching you."

"Good," says Corey.

But I don't think anything is good right now. I'm upset. If Chris is hurt, it's all my fault. I feel like crying. I reach in my pocket for my handkerchief. And all my reward money falls onto the ground at Dad's feet.

GET A GRIP, PIP!

CHAPTER 3

It's a bad, bad scene.
"Where did you get this money?" says Dad.
I think I'm going to get murdered right here on our lawn in front of the neighbors. Corey is clutching his pocket in case he has to give up his jelly beans. But Dad's eyes are on me.
"Seven dollars and twenty-five cents. Where did you get this money?" says Dad. "I'm waiting. Where did this come from?"
I'd like to say, "The State Treasury," but it'll get me into more trouble. So I get a grip and say nothing.
"Where did the money come from, Corey?"

27

Corey looks at Dad. Then he looks at me and presses his lips together firmly. I didn't know he was such a brave little kid.

"Ah," says Dad. "I suspect some sort of deal here between an innocent little five-year-old and a cunning big eleven-year-old."

That really gets on my nerves. One minute I'm a little girl and the next I'm a cunning big eleven-year-old. Dad changes the rules to suit himself.

He stares intently at Corey, who starts to shuffle and turn red.

"It's not Corey's fault," I say. "We earned this money honestly. We found a lost dog and we returned it."

As I'm speaking, I'm thinking. If I tell the whole story about Howard, Dad might put two and two together and connect Howard and Meatball. And Howard and the drainpipe. And Chris and the drainpipe. Then I might have to return lost cats and rabbits and tortoises and all sorts of livestock because not only will I be paying for a window and a drainpipe, but also for Chris's fractures and concussion.

"You can tell me as we drive," says Dad.

We head down the freeway toward the City Hospital.

"There's one!" says Corey.

"One what?" says Dad, his eyes following Corey's pointing finger.

There's a big, black dog, and it's marching purposefully down the sidewalk. It's not lost. It has that confident air of knowing exactly where it's going. Dad latches onto Corey's excitement like a blood-starved leech. I guess years of parenting give you this instinct. It's very highly developed in my dad.

"It's just a dog, Corey," he says, speaking in a deceptively calm voice.

GET A GRIP, PIP!

Not to Corey; in his tiny brain, it's a possible ten dollars on the paw. I nudge him, but it's too late.

"We need to take him back to his house," squeaks Corey, nose pushed flat against the window. "Then we might get a reward."

ACCIDENTAL EMERGENCY

There's an awful silence. Corey, suddenly aware that he's said something of national importance, looks bewildered. We slow to a crawl outside the hospital and Dad stops alongside a vacant parking space.

"Corey just means that we found that lost dog and took it back," I say. "And its owner gave us reward money."

Dad turns to look at me, which isn't a good idea when he's supposed to be doing a parallel park in reverse. Crunch! He hits a pole behind us with a thump. He grits his teeth and straightens the wheel, grinding the gears savagely. I'm scared he's going to go crazy right outside the hospital and be carted inside in a straitjacket. Corey is staring at me with a sad and sorry look.

"How many dogs?" says Dad.

"One," I say.

"Ten," says Corey. "It should've been ten but the others didn't want to come with us. So it was only one."

GET A GRIP, PIP!

"Out of the car," said Dad. "I'll deal with you later, Pip!"

"Does this mean we won't be going to the movies?" says Corey softly.

I roll my eyes skyward. I'll be lucky if I'm ever allowed to go to the movies again.

Dad walks around to the back of our car to inspect the damage. I look at the crumpled

metal and wonder dismally if he's going to blame this one on me, too.

How much will it cost to repair one "little" bump? Two, three hundred dollars? I think Dad's going to have a heart attack right there on the sidewalk but he just squares his shoulders and marches up the steps. We follow. We go into the emergency department. Chris has been checked out for any concussion; he's okay but has to rest for twenty-four hours. If he starts getting headaches, he has to return to the hospital, fast. He has to be kept calm and quiet. He's only sprained his wrist, and he has it bandaged.

He looks a bit pale and there are cat scratches on his good hand. But apart from the scratches and the bandage you'd never guess he'd taken a dive off a drainpipe. We can go home.

"I'm not exactly sure what happened this morning," says Dad, when we're finally home eating a late lunch, "but I think you were going to take people's dogs and return them for money. Is that it?"

"No! Well…"

"How could you, Pip?" Then Dad says that we'll be donating my seven dollars and twenty-five cents to the local animal shelter.

I can see my charity money slipping away and suggest we donate the money to needy kids instead of needy dogs. I'm about to tell him about the school charity drive, but he misses the point and thinks I'm talking about donating it to myself. I guess the frustrated look on my face doesn't help the situation. Time for a lecture on greed and how I should be thankful I've got a home, food, clothes... And I'm grounded for a week.

CHAPTER 4

FLOWER POWER

One thing about being grounded is that it gives you time to think. So, how can I make some more money? I think hard. Dogs – no, definitely not! But flowers, like the bunch I saw a boy carrying into the hospital; like the beautiful assortment I saw this morning growing in our neighbors' gardens – hanging over fences onto public property, just begging to be cut and made into lovely bouquets, decorated with little paper doilies and satin ribbon...

The trouble is, it's very difficult to operate a hands-on business like floral distribution

GET A GRIP, PIP!

when you're grounded for a week. But where there's a will there's a way, and I've definitely got the will, with the charity drive closing in little over a week. I'm still allowed to walk to school and back, so I'm going to have to walk very quickly.

FLOWER POWER

After school I tell Becky I have to get home (which is true), and I take a short cut across the park. I zip down the next street where I remember there are heaps of overhanging flowers. Snip, snip, snip with the scissors, and into a plastic bag go the flowers. I walk quickly past several bare yards and into the next street. Snip, snip, snip.

My plastic bag is soon bulging so I decide it's time to start work. I sit on the bench in a bus stop and swiftly assemble the flowers into bunches. A paper doily wrapped around the stems, a pretty ribbon, and I have ten bunches ready to sell.

GET A GRIP, PIP!

But where to sell them? Not door-to-door, because, knowing my luck, the first door I knock on will be opened by Dad, who will just happen to have been visiting a friend on his way home from work. Besides, it's far too dangerous.

I decide I need a soda, so I go into a store. It sells all sorts of things, even greeting cards. That's when I get a brilliant idea.

"I've noticed you have cards and chocolates to sell," I say to the owner. "Maybe people would like to buy flowers as well. I have some nice bouquets right here."

I give each bunch a little shake as I arrange them on the counter. The lady stares, then gets a funny, closed look on her face. But then I realize she's thinking about money, and the look on her face is just the result of her brain cells moving around.

"How much?" asks the lady.

How much? I think quickly.

"Four dollars a bunch."

She snorts and her lips purse.

"I'll give you one-fifty, and no more." She rattles around in the cash register and hands me fifteen dollars. "A dollar in the hand is worth two on the rose bush," she says.

Pretty weird.

FLOWER POWER

"Can you bring me some more tomorrow?" she says.

Wow, a regular customer! This is going to be easy. I'll pay off my debt by the end of the week *and* have time to catch up on the charity drive.

I go outside and stuff the money into my socks. This is so easy! Maybe the video store will buy some flowers, too. Maybe the dry cleaners; I could have a whole chain of outlets...

"Philippa Peppercorn! What are you doing here?"

GET A GRIP, PIP!

"Dad!"

He looks boiling mad. His car is parked right outside the store.

"Get in this car, now," he growls.

He's so mad he nearly has steam coming out of his nostrils. But on an Angry Scale of ten, Dad's only a six, and I soar to a nine when the lady from the store comes out with my flowers in a bucket and a sign that reads: "Fresh flowers. Four dollars a bunch."

Talk about ripped off!

CHAPTER 5

OUT OF LUCK

"Hi, Pete," the lady says to Dad.

"Hello, Lorraine. I'll be right in," says Dad, opening the car door.

I bolt into the back seat and hide my face. Out of the corner of my eye I can see Dad and the lady talking. She's gazing up at him with this sparkly look in her eyes that lots of women give my dad. I hope he doesn't ask her out on a date and then buy her a bunch of my flowers!

I'm starting to feel that I've really lost my grip this time. How can one person have such rotten luck? And how am I supposed to know

GET A GRIP, PIP!

that Dad stops by that particular store every night for his evening paper on his way home from work? He grimly tells me this as we roar down the road, after Lorraine, still sparkling, has leaned into our car, batted her eyelashes, and reminded me to bring her some more flowers.

Dad has totally lost his temper. "I've taught you not to steal," he shouts, as we race down the home straight.

"It wasn't stealing," I argue. "If stuff is growing along the street, then isn't it public property?"

Dad gives a strangled groan.

"Inside, and start dinner," he snaps. "And now you're grounded for another week."

Great. The way I'm going, I'll be twenty by the time I'm ungrounded and allowed to go on my first date. The only good thing is that Dad hasn't noticed the flower money. I've stuffed it down my socks – and on Monday it's going to be the start of the Pip Peppercorn charity contribution at school. Now I have to get to my room and hide it. I can tie little rolls of it up with thread and push them into the air vent in my room. Dad'll never notice the strands of thread dangling down.

Chris is parked in front of the TV. He's spilled corn chips all over the floor and there's a pool of liquid where his drink has slopped on the coffee table. As soon as Dad and I walk through the door he gets his feet off the sofa and tries to look frail. And does Dad yell at him about the mess he's made? No way. He asks Chris how he's feeling and tells him to rest up.

Chris looks toward me, then his eyes narrow suspiciously. "Pip's got money stuffed in her socks," he says.

I will creep into his room in the dead of night and plant a virus in his computer, I tell myself.

"Take off your socks," says Dad.

"No."

"Do it!" When Dad gets that tone in his voice, there's no arguing. He grabs the money and stuffs it in his pocket.

"Pip, this is the last time. Do you hear me? No more. And you're grounded for a month."

"It's not fair. I'm getting grounded twice for the same thing." But it's no use. Dad's too mad to listen.

OUT OF LUCK

Maybe I should run away. But I'd need money. And where would I go? I'm trapped in my own house. We eat dinner, grilled steak and salad. Then I go to my room. No TV. No phone calls. No friends. I may as well be on the moon!

GET A GRIP, PIP!

The next day at school I'm on staff-room duty, which means I have to put out cups and saucers and pile cookies on plates, ready for the teachers' morning break. The woman in the office used to do it but she's too busy now, so kids have to do it. It's child labor. And we're not about to take a cookie in case Mr. Blitheroe has "wired" them with microchips to alert him if a cookie goes missing before ten o'clock.

Then I go out for the morning assembly and announcements. Sean Doppermail has won Student of the Month for being "most caring kid" in the school. The way I'm going, he'll probably win the charity plaque, too. I'm beginning to think that maybe I should join his group of friends; it must be nice never to be in trouble. Nice, but boring. Mr. Blitheroe is talking away, something about lunch orders, garbage messing up the grounds, lost coats, lost books, and a lost dog named Hairy, but I'm not really listening. After this exciting extravaganza we go to our classrooms.

We have reading followed by math. I'm very quiet. My teacher, Ms. Paldini, asks if I'm all right. "My spirit is broken," I say dramatically, but she just rolls her eyes to the ceiling while everyone (except Becky) laughs. I can see that it's going to be another great day.

At recess there is a notice on the board about the lost dog. Since the announcement, I can't help thinking that it's named "Hairy." This is actually spelled "Hari," which looks very exotic. It's a cream-colored Beluki hound and it must be valuable because the reward is two hundred dollars. I stare at the board. Two hundred dollars is a lot of money.

This dog must be somewhere in town. I make up my mind to go on a mission to find Hairy, alias Hari.

GET A GRIP, PIP!

I'm ungrounded for an hour and a half right after school, because I have to play basketball. Dad would've grounded me for the entire match except that I'm the highest scorer on the team and the other parents would never talk to him again if I wasn't allowed to play. As we walk across the park to the basketball court, I keep an eye open for Hairy, but there's only a big, black dog with a head like a squashed bug, and a little fluffy white dog that looks like someone's bedroom slipper.

We play our game and win. Yeah team! I've played a good game and managed to stay cool – without doing anything dumb. And the way things have been lately, that's a big achievement.

"Want to go for a milkshake?" says Becky.

I think about this. With my luck, I'm bound to do something disastrous and be grounded for eternity.

"Nah. I'll pass."

"See you."

I head off along the side of the park. I could cut across but I'm supposed to go the long way around, keeping to the paths in case I meet a stranger. I keep a wary eye on the trees and skirt the edge of the bushes. Then I hear a rustling noise and my muscles tense, ready for flight.

Zap! A dog with creamy, long fur bounces out. It stops when it sees me, growling low in its throat. The fur on its back stands straight up like my shaggy-dog toothbrush. It looks at me carefully from its strange, yellowish eyes and I stare back. Then it gives a low whine and sinks onto its belly, crawling along the ground toward me. It looks very thin and very hungry.

"Hairy?"

The dog gives a whimper and wriggles right up to me. I can't believe it – Hairy in the flesh! Two hundred dollars' worth of dog and my ticket to a debt-free existence and charity drive success.

"Come on," I say, "I'll take you to your owner."

OUT OF LUCK

But Hairy just whimpers some more, then makes a lunge at my arm. I freeze. He's decided it's time for dinner and I'm on the menu. I shut my eyes and try to scream but it's sort of strangled in my throat.

Surprisingly, Hairy's jaws don't bite my flesh; they tug at my sleeve. I open my eyes. He tugs again.

"You want me to follow you, Hairy?"

He turns and trots back into the bushes, so I follow. Now what?

CHAPTER 6

HAIRY'S FRIEND

Hairy disappears into a thick bush. I get down on my hands and knees and crawl after him. There's a low growl, then more whimpering. I part the bush and find myself peering into a pair of gentle brown eyes. They belong to the dirtiest, scruffiest dog I've ever seen. It's got a peculiar square head. The whole dog looks like a scrub brush with half the bristles missing, matted with mud, and tangled with burrs and grass. And it seems to have a sore paw.

"Oh, you poor thing."

GET A GRIP, PIP!

I reach in and gently pick up the dog. I think it's a girl. It looks like a girl. She licks my hand very gently while Hairy looks anxious.

"It's okay. You can both come home with me," I say.

I carry the little, dirty, gray dog carefully while Hairy lopes alongside, lifting his paws daintily like a show pony. Yes, you can always tell breeding. This cream dog obviously has a pedigree a mile long. The poor little dog is just a mutt, but she's so cute. When this little gray lady has some dinner, I'll give her a bath, and then Dad might let me keep her. It won't be so bad being grounded for life if I have my own dog.

When I get home, I decide I'd better put them both in the garage while I get them some food. I have to bathe Gray Lady's paw. I leave them together on some old blankets while I get bowls for food and water.

We don't have any dog food, so I open some canned beef stew. At the same time I check out the Lost and Found column in today's paper. Hairy's in there, but no gray dog. Maybe I should call the animal shelter and find out if anyone's lost her. I take the food out to Hairy and Gray Lady and while they wolf it down I go back for a basin and cloth to wash Gray Lady's sore paw. I make a quick phone call and the man at the shelter tells me that no one has reported losing a shaggy, dirty, grayish dog. I don't ask about Hairy because he'd probably drive out, collect him and claim the reward himself.

GET A GRIP, PIP!

I finally have a grip on the situation and I know exactly what to do. I go back out to the garage and they're lying side by side with full bellies and happy expressions.

"I'll try not to hurt you," I say to Gray Lady as I bathe her paw gently. Hairy watches anxiously. Then it hits me – they're in love. It's so romantic. It makes me feel all...

"Pip!" bellows Dad, and I nearly jump through the roof. "Where are you?"

I look at Hairy and Gray Lady. No choice – I'll have to show Dad. So I yell out and tell him I'm in the garage. As his footsteps approach, Hairy growls deep in his throat. I give him a pat and he quiets down.

"What...?"

"Look, Dad. Hairy."

"What?"

"A lost dog. Hairy. I found him. And, Dad, there's a two hundred dollar reward."

"Well, well, well. And how do you know that, Pip?"

So I explain about Mr. Blitheroe and the reward notice.

"And this other dog?"

"That's his girlfriend, Gray Lady. Dad, do you think – if no one's looking for her...? Dad, I rang the animal shelter, and it looks like she needs a home. Do you think I could keep her? She'll be really cute once I've bathed her, and she's very gentle. I'll take care of her myself, I promise."

"A dog? Living here?"

"Please, Dad. It'll... help me be GOOD."

Dad laughs. "All right, Pip. If no one owns the gray dog you can keep her. But we'd better call about the cream one right away. The owner must be very worried."

So I stay with Hairy and Gray Lady while Dad goes inside to call. The two hundred dollar reward will pay off all my debts, and give me a good start towards the charity drive, but I feel sad. Hairy and Gray Lady will be away from each other. Maybe Hairy's owner will let them visit. I'll ask.

"The man will be here soon," says Dad, coming back. "You'd better eat your dinner, Pip. It's getting cold."

But I'm too excited to eat, and when I hear a car pull into our driveway I leap to my feet and rush to the door, flinging it open as a short, chubby man gets out.

"Philippa Peppercorn!"

"Mr. Blitheroe."

We stare at each other. Mr. Blitheroe looks annoyed. "If this is some sort of joke…"

"It's not a joke. I found Hairy in the park, and now he's in the garage."

"He? My dog's a female."

I look at Dad. Maybe Hairy is a female.

"Come this way, Mr. Blitheroe," says Dad.

We all walk down to the garage. Hairy appears in the door and looks at Mr. Blitheroe suspiciously.

"This isn't my dog. This is just a mongrel," says Mr. Blitheroe angrily to Dad. "Can't you tell a pedigreed dog from a mutt?"

"No, I can't," says Dad, in the deceptively quiet voice he uses when he's annoyed, "I know very little about dogs…"

But then the strangest thing happens. Gray Lady comes running out looking excited. She gives an excited little yip and tries to jump up.

"My Hari," says Mr. Blitheroe, and scoops her into his arms.

HAIRY'S FRIEND

Dad and I stare. We blink in amazement. "But... she's not a creamy color," I say, totally stunned.

"Yes she is – when she's clean," says Mr. Blitheroe in a very cold voice. "*And* she is a very rare breed, worth well over a thousand dollars. I don't know what you've been doing

GET A GRIP, PIP!

to my dog or why you didn't call me sooner. But I suspect that Pip has kept her tied up here in this garage, as some strange sort of joke. I've a good mind to call the police. You'll certainly get no reward from me."

"Stop right there, Mr. Blitheroe," says Dad. He turns to look at me. "Pip, where and when did you find these dogs?"

"Like I said, today after basketball in the park."

Dad turns to Mr. Blitheroe. "My daughter's telling the truth. I can always tell if she's fibbing."

I nearly faint on the spot. He can tell? Well, that's the end of any more extensions of the truth, then. I'd already decided that, anyway – after recent events.

"And," continues Dad, "I was going to tell you to forget the reward. Pip was doing you a favor. But in the light of what you've just said, you can write her a check for two hundred dollars right now, or the dog stays here. I'm sure, Mr. Blitheroe, that a man of your esteem and standing in this town would not break a promise…"

So Mr. Blitheroe reluctantly writes a check payable to P. Peppercorn. Then he takes Hari and drives off in a big huff. Too bad.

HAIRY'S FRIEND

Dad and I had a big laugh – the first we'd had together in ages. Daringly, I told him all about why I was so desperate to raise money, and instead of getting upset again he seemed pretty impressed. He's canceled my debt and I'm giving the check to the charity drive on Monday. Unreal. And instead of keeping Gray Lady (who's really Hari the Fourth), I'm keeping Hairy Peppercorn the First – if no one answers the Found notice that we're going to put in the paper. I'm hoping that I'll be able to take Hairy to see his girlfriend sometimes – but somehow I don't think I'll be suggesting that to Mr. Blitheroe for a little while yet.

In the meantime, I can't wait until Mr. Blitheroe has to hand me that plaque at the assembly next week – though really I don't even mind if Sean Doppermail wins it instead. Dad's on my side, and even Chris has had to admit that maybe I'm not so bad after all. Suddenly life is looking GREAT!

TITLES IN THE SERIES

SET 9A

Television Drama
Time for Sale
The Shady Deal
The Loch Ness Monster Mystery
Secrets of the Desert

SET 9B

To JJ From CC
Pandora's Box
The Birthday Disaster
The Song of the Mantis
Helping the Hoiho

SET 9C

Glumly
Rupert and the Griffin
The Tree, the Trunk, and the Tuba
Errol the Peril
Cassidy's Magic

SET 9D

Barney
Get a Grip, Pip!
Casey's Case
Dear Future
Strange Meetings

SET 10A

A Battle of Words
The Rainbow Solution
Fortune's Friend
Eureka
It's a Frog's Life

SET 10B

The Cat Burglar of Pethaven Drive
The Matchbox
In Search of the Great Bears
Many Happy Returns
Spider Relatives

SET 10C

Horrible Hank
Brian's Brilliant Career
Fernitickles
It's All in Your Mind,
    James Robert
Wing High, Gooftah

SET 10D

The Week of the Jellyhoppers
Timothy Whuffenpuffen-
    Whippersnapper
Timedetectors
Ryan's Dog Ringo
The Secret of Kiribu Tapu Lagoon